CHINA DOLL

CHINADOLL

Marjorie Chan

China Doll
first published 2004 by
Scirocco Drama
An imprint of J. Gordon Shillingford Publishing Inc.
©2004 Marjorie Chan
Reprinted June 2009

Scirocco Drama Series Editor: Glenda MacFarlane
Cover design by Doowah Design Inc.
Author photo by Pierre Gautreau
Production and cover photos by John Lauener
Printed and bound in Canada on 100% post-consumer recycled paper.

We acknowledge the financial support of the Manitoba Arts Council, The Canada
Council for the Arts and the Government of Canada through the Book Publishing
Industry Development Program (BPIDP) for our publishing program.

Canadian Cataloguing in Publication Data

Chan, Marjorie
        China doll/Marjorie Chan.
A play.
ISBN 0-920486-83-5

I. Title.
PS8605.H355C45 2004   C812'.6   C2004-904917-8

J. Gordon Shillingford Publishing
P.O. Box 86, RPO Corydon Avenue, Winnipeg, MB Canada R3M 3S3

Acknowledgements

I am extremely grateful for the support of many people in the writing of this play. In particular, I would like to thank:
Kelly Thornton, for her incredible faith and vision.
Bill Lane, Dagmar Kaffanke-Nunn, Lynda Hill, Ruth Madoc-Jones, Erica Kopyto, Jennifer Capraru, Jordana Commisso, Reni Krátká, The Butterfly Body Collective, The K.M. Hunter Foundation, David and Ann Powell, Linda Gaboriau, and John Murrell for their support, dramaturgical and otherwise.
And finally my family, Janet and Edwin Chan, Jennifer Chan, and Parveen Bakshi for their love.

Development History

China Doll was first commissioned by Bill Lane as a short radio drama for CBC Radio and the Banff Centre of the Arts. It was then commissioned as a full-length play by Kelly Thornton for Nightwood Theatre. It was subsequently developed through the 2003 Groundswell Festival and the 2003 Banff playRites Colony and supported by a Creation Grant from The Canada Council for the Arts.

The playwright would also like to acknowledge all the performers who participated in various versions and workshops for their invaluable contribution: Denis Akiyama, Leanna Brodie, Lindsay Burns, Jo Chim, Jordana Commisso, Brian Dooley, Barbara Gates-Wilson, Carmen Grant, Laura Kim, Paul Sun-Hyung Lee, David Lereaney, Keira Loughran, Jane Luk, Ruth Madoc-Jones, John Ng, Valerie Pearson, Meg Roe, Jovanni Sy, Jean Yoon.

Note from the Playwright

China Doll was inspired by the 2001 exhibit "Every Step a Lotus" at the Bata Shoe Museum. It was there that I encountered these exquisitely embroidered but painfully small 'lotus' shoes. I was astonished to discover the wear on the soles of the shoes could only have been caused by walking. I had always imagined that women with bound feet could not possibly walk anywhere. But they did.

Characters

Su-Ling
Ma-Ma, *her mother*
Poa-Poa, *Ma-Ma's mother, and Su-Ling's grandmother*
Merchant Li
Ming, *Su-Ling's servant*

Act I is set in Shanghai, China 1904–1918, returning occasionally to the past in a nearby village.

Act II is set over a few weeks in the fall of 1918 at the Chen compound, Shanghai.

On a style note, I encourage directors to interpret freely the images I provide in stage directions, including incorporating other theatrical forms such as dance or puppetry etc. In particular, scenes with foot-binding and sexual content are better served stylized. I would also encourage intense research into this particular period in China's cultural and political history. However, more important than a naturalistic portrayal of the time period, is the essence of the story, fluidity and a sense of magic.

Notes on the Text

Su-Ling reads from excerpts of literature of my own creation, with the exception of the excerpt from *A Doll's House* by Henrik Ibsen in Act II, Scene 8. The text she reads is based on the William Archer (1856-1924) translation from 1906 which is in the public domain. I made my own further amendments for clarity and rhythm.

Production History

China Doll was commissioned and first produced by Nightwood Theatre, premiering at the Tarragon Theatre Extra Space, Toronto, February 19, 2004. The cast and crew were as follows:

SU-LING .... Marjorie Chan
POA-POA .... Jo Chim
MING/MA-MA .... Keira Loughran
MERCHANT LI .... John Ng

Directed and Dramaturged by Kelly Thornton
Artistic Producer: Nathalie Bonjour
Set and Costume Designer: Joanne Dente
Associate Designer: Camellia Koo
Lighting Designers: Rebecca Picherack and Michelle Ramsay
Sound Designer: Richard Lee
Stage Manager: Kathryn Westoll
Assistant Stage Manager: Sarah Dalgleish
Production Managers: Rebecca Picherack and Michelle Ramsay
Assistant Director/Dramaturge: Erica Kopyto
Fight Director: Richard Lee
Movement Coach: Kelly McEvenue
Head of Wardrobe: Barbara Rowe
Lotus Shoe Construction: Sarah Rotering
Scenic Artist: Julie Ekness
Carpenters: Bill Stahl, Will Sutton
House Technician: Gavin Fearon
Administrative Assistant: Natasha Mytnowych

China Doll was nominated for three 2004 Dora Mavor Moore Awards in the General Theatre Category, Outstanding Costume Design, Outstanding Production and Outstanding New Play.

Marjorie Chan

Marjorie is a writer and actor based in Toronto. A graduate of George Brown Theatre School, she has performed across the country from Vancouver to New Brunswick.

China Doll is her debut as a playwright and began as a short radio drama for the Banff Centre and CBC Radio. Marjorie's other dramas for CBC Radio include *In a Heartbeat, Rabbit Box* and *Spring Arrival*. The premiere of her short opera *Mother Everest* (with composer Abigail Richardson) was commissioned and produced by Tapestry New Opera Works as a part of their innovative "Opera To Go." As a writer, she has participated in the Deep Wireless Radio Theatre Ensemble (New Adventures in Sound Art), Factory Theatre Playwrights' Lab, The Radiophonic Workshops (CBC Radio/Banff Centre), playRites Colony (Banff Centre), Groundswell Festivals (Nightwood Theatre), Librettist/Composer Laboratory (Tapestry New Opera Works), as well as being Playwright-in-Residence for Theatre Direct Canada. She has been awarded the 2004 K.M. Hunter Artist Award in Theatre and nominated for several Dora Mavor Moore Awards both as an actor and a writer, winning for Outstanding Performance in Theatre for Young Audiences. Her next play is entitled *Sweet Protest* and is set in Toronto, 1947.

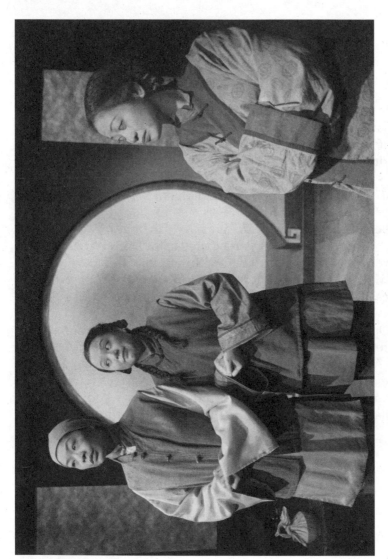

Poa-Poa (Jo Chim), Su-Ling (Marjorie Chan) and Ma-Ma (Keira Loughran)

Act I

Scene 1 Prologue 1918 (1904)

> *Enter SU-LING (16), wearing rags and with her feet unbound. She is in a courtyard, it is snowing.*

SU-LING: I am walking into the future...

> *She crosses the stage unsteadily but with determination.*
>
> *Behind SU-LING, her mother, MA-MA appears as if in a memory. She is teaching SU-LING as a toddler how to walk.*

MA-MA: *(A made-up song in a period Chinese style.)*

Su-Ling-Ling. Who is smiling?

Su-Ling-Ling. Who is laughing?

Su-Ling-Ling. Who is walking?

> *POA-POA, SU-LING's maternal grandmother appears, also a memory.*

POA-POA: Hua-Ling, don't coddle her. She must learn on her own.

MA-MA: But Ma-Ma, she's just a baby!

POA-POA: Let go of her! See what she can do!

MA-MA: I don't want her to fall.

POA-POA: If she falls down...so be it.

MA-MA: Ma-Ma!

POA-POA: She'll have to stand on her own two feet one day.

> MA-MA *lets go of the baby, who walks towards*
> *POA-POA.*

MA-MA: She's walking! My little girl! I wish your father was
              home to see this…

POA-POA: Yes. Well. Never mind. Little Ling-Ling! Come to
              me, come to your grandmother!

MA-MA: Su-Ling… Say bye to your Ma-Ma! Say bye-bye!

SU-LING (16): Goodbye Ma-Ma.

> MA-MA *disappears into the past.*

Scene 2 1907

> SU-LING *is five years old.* POA-POA *is binding*
> SU-LING's *feet.* SU-LING *is remote, as if*
> *remembering and not directly experiencing.*

POA-POA: Su-Ling. Today is the day to bind your feet. I'm
              going wrap the bandages around your toes. All of
              them except your big toe. He gets to stay free. This
              part doesn't hurt a bit.

> POA-POA *wraps bindings around* SU-LING's
> *entire foot.*

See? What did I say? We want your feet to stay this
size forever! Look at mine! I was five too, when my
feet were bound! Like little Yexian. You remember
the story of Yexian…

> SU-LING *nods.*

You have to be brave for the next part. I'm going to
take this bandage and use it to pull your toes. I'm
going to pull your toes, back under your feet. Like
this.

> *POA-POA demonstrates by curling her fingers into her palm.*

When I pull, it will hurt. I will have to pull very hard. Ready?

> *POA-POA pulls her toes toward the heels. SU-LING is suddenly present in the scene, screaming.*

SU-LING: Aaaaaaah! *(Continuing under POA-POA's speech.)*

POA-POA: *(Each pause an exertion in the binding.)* For any–proper–family to consider–you–as a–bride— You–must have–the best–and tiniest–lotus feet...

> *The screaming subsides.*

We have so little else.

Scene 3 1909

> *Shanghai. SU-LING and POA-POA's one-room apartment dominated by a kang (Chinese style heated bed). Some attempt has been made to dress it up with hangings, though they are worn and have seen better days. Both SU-LING and POA-POA are neatly dressed but in shabby clothes. The only visible object of worth is POA-POA's ornate cane. SU-LING is still recovering from her binding and experiences pain when she walks. The noise of a big city and a marching protest in the distance.*

POA-POA: Su-Ling! Get away from the window!

SU-LING (7): I want to see!

POA-POA: There's nothing to see! The water for the tea should be ready.

SU-LING: Yes, Poa-Poa.

POA-POA: That's a good child... Taking care of your grandmother. Your mother was never this way...too busy dreaming. But better than your idiot father! He only had a nose for gambling and smoking, no wonder he died in an opium—

SU-LING: *(Interrupting.)* Here's your tea.

POA-POA: Aren't there any buns?

SU-LING: They're all gone.

             Beat.

POA-POA: We used to have as many buns as we wanted... Remember our old house in the village. Remember the garden, and the little pond! We would sit and you would stare into it. Waiting for Yexian's carp to come and speak with you!

SU-LING: Yes, Poa-Poa.

POA-POA: Now look at me! Up at dawn! To sew for the Chens! You should see their houses. Courtyard after courtyard.

SU-LING: Can I come and see the Chen houses?

POA-POA: Of course not.

SU-LING: Why not?

POA-POA: Don't talk back to me. Let me see your sewing.

SU-LING: Yes, Poa-Poa.

             SU-LING shows her a sampler swatch.

POA-POA: No. They are still not even. Do you see? Here. And here. Try again.

SU-LING: Yes, Poa-Poa.

             POA-POA puts the fire in the stove out.

POA-POA: And don't start the fire again.

SU-LING: But it's cold!

POA-POA: You're too young. You could burn everything down.

              *POA-POA exits. SU-LING starts to sew, but
              becomes frustrated. She plays instead with the bits of
              fabric.*

SU-LING: Hello...magical carp! Today I want roasted duck
              and snow pea leaves and and...and an orange!

              *She closes her eyes and then with one eye barely
              peeking, she arranges the tea beside her on the bed-
              couch. Then she opens her eyes, feigning surprise.*

              You did it! Thank you, magical carp!

              *Like magic, a real carp appears, along with a small
              orange. SU-LING picks it up eagerly and begins to
              eat it.*

Scene 4 (Flashback) 1906

              *MA-MA and SU-LING are in the village courtyard,
              eating oranges. SU-LING spits out the seeds.*

MA-MA: Little one! Stop that... Don't spit those on the
              ground! Where are your manners?

SU-LING (4): But I don't want them!

MA-MA: You can save them. Here, place them here. We'll
              soak the seeds. Then together, we'll watch the tree
              grow!

SU-LING: Ba-Ba too?

MA-MA: Yes...all together. Like a family.

SU-LING: When is Ba-Ba coming back?

MA-MA: Soon, hopefully tomorrow. Now, where shall we
              plant the tree when it gets big enough?

SU-LING: But Ma-Ma, it's so small!

MA-MA: What is? The seed?

SU-LING: How does a big tree get inside?

MA-MA: It isn't inside. Just the beginning of it. Then it grows from small to big!

SU-LING: Did I come from a seed?

MA-MA: Well, yes, in a manner of speaking.

SU-LING: Ma-Ma, did I grow from my baby toe?

MA-MA: Yes...yes you did!

Scene 5 1911

Though SU-LING's (9) feet are bound, the worst is past and she has discovered great mobility. They are in a Shanghai shop, a jumble of assorted household items, but mostly fabrics and things associated with sewing. There is also a curtain which leads to a back room. MERCHANT LI enters. He is middle-aged with an enigmatic air. He is carrying a selection of impressive fabrics.

MERCHANT LI: (*Hostile.*) We are so happy the Chens continue to send their fair representative to us.

POA-POA: At least someone is happy about that.

MERCHANT LI: If you could... I don't like children in my store.

POA-POA: My granddaughter, Su-Ling.

MERCHANT LI: She can wait outside.

POA-POA: It's too dangerous in the streets. (*Off his look.*) She won't bother us.

MERCHANT LI: See to it that she doesn't touch anything.

POA-POA: Don't worry, Merchant Li, she has proper manners. Go ahead.

SU-LING: Honourable Merchant Li.

MERCHANT LI: Uh, hello. *(To POA-POA.)* I thought she would have
                 the same name as her mother.

POA-POA: Excuse me?

MERCHANT LI: Oh no, of course!

                 (Very pointedly.) It's concubine's daughters that are
                 given the same name.

POA-POA: Merchant Li—

MERCHANT LI: Why don't you have a look at these? I'm sure that
                 one of them is good enough for the Chens.

POA-POA: Perhaps. Is this one very expensive?

SU-LING: It has to be. It's the nicest one here!

POA-POA: I said to say nothing!

MERCHANT LI: This one is of the highest quality. Look at the
                 weaving here. Have you ever seen such edges? The
                 quality of the silk, the very best.

POA-POA: It is soft.

                 *She reaches for the cloth, but MERCHANT LI pulls
                 it away.*

MERCHANT LI: Are you sure that the Chens have authorized you so
                 much credit?

POA-POA: The Chens trust my judgement!

MERCHANT LI: Indeed.

POA-POA: I'm not interested in that one, anyway! It looks a bit
                 too showy for them.

MERCHANT LI: Of course. How about this one?

                 Noise. Political upheaval. Protesters chanting.

SU-LING: What's happening?

POA-POA: Those troublemakers! No doubt friends of yours?

MERCHANT LI: You still refuse to believe that it is a new beginning!

POA-POA: What of the Emperor Pu-Yi!

MERCHANT LI: He's five years old! You expect a child to run China! No, the time for a Republic is ripe, where people can choose freely—

POA-POA: Choose freely! I can't even choose a fabric without a lecture!

MERCHANT LI: But Sun Yat-Sen, he could be China's future! Think of her!

POA-POA: Merchant Li! Are you quite finished? I did not bring my granddaughter here to listen to your politics, filling her head with nonsense. Is this a shop or not? Because if not, we should do better to head down the street.

MERCHANT LI: My deepest apologies. This is indeed a respectable establishment.

POA-POA: Is it?

> POA-POA picks up the very first piece of expensive cloth.

POA-POA: Your merchandise is shoddy. Low quality. This ugly thing. It can't be worth very much.

MERCHANT LI: No you're right, it is very badly woven.

SU-LING: That's not what you said before…

MERCHANT LI: Your grandmother is right. She's always right. Don't forget that!

SU-LING: Oh. *(Thinks a bit.)* Everything, everything in this shop is shit!

POA-POA: Su-Ling! *(To MERCHANT LI.)* Well? What are you waiting for? Are you going to cut the fabric or not?

Scene 6 1911

Their apartment in Shanghai, after returning home from MERCHANT LI's shop. POA-POA agitated and binds SU-LING's feet during this scene.

POA-POA: How dare you? How dare you behave that way! I told you to say nothing! I told you to be quiet! I've never been so embarrassed in my life! Haven't I raised you to be a lady? Don't I spend all my time taking care of you?

SU-LING: Yes.

POA-POA: Then why? Why act like an ill-mannered idiot? In front of him, no less! Do you know who that man is? Do you? He's from our village. He knows about everything! And every chance he gets he tries to shove it in my face! Every week I have to go in there and see his smirk! "Have the Chens authorized you so much credit?" The Chens entrust me with that and much much more!

SU-LING: I know!

POA-POA: We can't let these people get in our way! Their looks, their snide remarks! I hate it, I hate it!

SU-LING: Yes, Poa-Poa.

POA-POA: "It's concubine's daughters that are given the same name!" How dare he bring that up! Every time I took a walk in the courtyard, servants would giggle, and the other children would point! "Look at Tien-Mei! Why would Master keep her around! Her Ma-Ma ran away to the teahouses, to serve men! One master obviously wasn't enough for her!"

SU-LING: They said that?

POA-POA: Not to my face, never to my face. But I heard them.

POA-POA finishes the binding.

POA-POA: My mother did one thing right. My feet were the smallest in the compound. In marriage, I made my escape, as a proper First Wife with my own house! And at least I was happy for a time.

SU-LING: What about your Ma-Ma?

POA-POA: Once, she hired a scribe and sent me a letter...

SU-LING: What did it say?

POA-POA: What did it say? What does it matter! As soon as my father handed it to me, I put the letter in the fire and watched it burn. Then I left my father's house with my head held high. Hold your head high Su-Ling, and you will survive.

SU-LING: Yes Poa-Poa.

POA-POA: We can't listen to what people might say. We only have each other. You trust me don't you?

SU-LING: Yes.

POA-POA: What did I say about your feet? Didn't I say they'd heal? They don't hurt as much anymore, do they?

SU-LING: No.

POA-POA: See? No matter what, you are my granddaughter and we will find a house for us, a marriage to give us a future. Your bindings, mind you keep them tight! Your feet are a good size and shape now. How could any man resist?

Scene 7 1912

MERCHANT LI's shop. SU-LING finds a book.

SU-LING (10): Poa-Poa, look!

POA-POA: What use is that!

SU-LING: Look at all the characters! What do these ones mean?

POA-POA does not know.

POA-POA: Put it down. A book won't help you sew your shoes!

SU-LING: I like it.

POA-POA: Put it down! Or you'll go home!

*SU-LING glowers and slips the book into her sleeve
without POA-POA seeing. MERCHANT LI enters.*

POA-POA: Ah, Merchant Li. Do you always keep your shop
unattended? Or does your Republic not have any
thieves?

MERCHANT LI: A true republic does not.

POA-POA: Apparently, a true republic is won on the backs of
others. While some choose to drink tea in their
shops.

MERCHANT LI: Some choose to wear cotton, and spin tales of silk.
Here to order fabrics for the house of Chen?

POA-POA: No. We're here to look at your lotus shoe patterns.

MERCHANT LI: Your first pair? You'll need to sew your engagement
shoes soon. You're almost old enough to marry right
now.

SU-LING: I'm only ten!

POA-POA: Merchant Li. When the time does come, I will be sure
to take care in my decision. The right husband for
Su-Ling would have to come from the very best of
families.

MERCHANT LI: Your granddaughter deserves no less.

POA-POA: Exactly. We'll want a simple pattern, as she's just
started to learn. Perhaps she could embroider a
lotus.

*MERCHANT LI rifles through the patterns
excitedly.*

MERCHANT LI: Good choice. Lotus represents purity. I think they would look wonderful, on your tiny feet.

SU-LING: No.

MERCHANT LI: How about these curly-eared bats?

SU-LING: No.

MERCHANT LI: I have just the design for you. Symbol of longevity. The butterfly.

SU-LING: No!

MERCHANT LI: See how pretty it is on the sole? You could embroider some trees with it...

SU-LING: Not a butterfly!

POA-POA: You have to choose something.

SU-LING: NO! I said no stupid butterflies. I hate them! You know I hate them!

> *Her outburst becomes a physical reality. A tantrum of fabric flies across the stage.*

Scene 8 (Flashback) 1907

> *House in the village, courtyard. A butterfly.*

SU-LING (5):   Poa-Poa! It that a flower?

POA-POA: Where?

SU-LING: Up there! A flower that can fly?

POA-POA: No, it's not a plant. It's a bug, with wings. Perhaps it will bring us luck.

SU-LING: Look at me! I'm a flying flower! I'm going to fly away!

POA-POA: Su-Ling. We are in mourning for your father. Show some respect.

SU-LING: I hate Ba-Ba. I hate him!

POA-POA: Don't say that. You should honour your ancestors.

SU-LING: But he made Ma-Ma so sad.

POA-POA: I know.

SU-LING: All she does is cry all the time.

POA-POA: She seems better today. She even took a walk in the gardens this morning.

SU-LING: *(Pointing.)* There it is again…

POA-POA: Wait… Ling-Ling…

SU-LING: Can I climb the tree?

POA-POA: Don't look Su-Ling…

> SU-LING *looks up at her mother's body hanging in the cypress tree.*

SU-LING: Ma-Ma?

POA-POA: Come on… Let's go…

SU-LING: Why are you in the tree like that? Ma-Ma?

> *A pair of white lotus shoes fall and remain suspended.*

Scene 9 Small Step 1912

> MERCHANT LI's shop. Hard rain. A thunderstorm brewing.

MERCHANT LI: What are you doing out alone? Does your grandmother know where you are?

SU-LING (10): No.

MERCHANT LI: I thought I would not see you again after your little tantrum. I suppose you bought your lotus shoe patterns at another shop?

SU-LING: Yes.

MERCHANT LI: Well. There's nothing I like more than to see your grandmother happy, though she probably paid too much...

                Low thunder in the distance.

                Is there something you wanted to say?

                No answer.

                No. Well then fine. Get on your way. I don't need any more outbursts from you.

SU-LING: I stole something.

MERCHANT LI: Ah. Your guilty conscience has finally caught up with you. Hand it over.

                She takes the book from her sleeve or pocket.

                Well, at least you had the sense to keep it dry.

SU-LING: I'm sorry.

MERCHANT LI: About what? Tell me, little girl, what exactly are you sorry for? Are you sorry that you embarrassed me in front of your grandmother? Are you sorry that you stole my book? Are you sorry that you ruined my merchandise? Which of these are you sorry for?

SU-LING: *(At a loss.)* Yes.

MERCHANT LI: That's it! Get out! I don't want you in my shop!

SU-LING: But it's raining so hard.

MERCHANT LI: Then walk down to an umbrella shop, and buy yourself an umbrella! You're not staying here!

SU-LING: I don't have any money.

MERCHANT LI: Then get wet. Come on, get out.

SU-LING: But it's cold.

Bright lightning, followed by thunder very close.

Please.

MERCHANT LI: Just this once! And only until the storm has passed!

He goes back to organizing fabrics. She saunters over to have a look.

No, no no no no. Stand over there.

She does so but fidgets.

Stop it. I'm not paying attention to you.

SU-LING: Don't you want to know what pattern I picked for my shoes?

MERCHANT LI: What pattern did you pick for your shoes?

SU-LING: A golden carp. Like Yexian's.

MERCHANT LI: *(Under his breath.)* Suits you.

SU-LING: What did you say?

MERCHANT LI: The carp. It suits you. Haven't you heard of the saying, "A carp swimming upstream never gives up" —even if it dies!

SU-LING: Can I sit down?

MERCHANT LI: Fine. Just be quiet!

She sits but stands up suddenly.

Now what?!

SU-LING: I have to pee.

MERCHANT LI: In the backroom...

She runs off.

And don't touch anything!

He continues with his work. SU-LING returns and MERCHANT LI looks up.

SU-LING: I didn't touch anything!

MERCHANT LI: Just sit down.

                She sits and finding the book again, she flips through
                casually.

                It's upside down. Didn't you know that?

SU-LING: Yes I know.

MERCHANT LI: Did you now?

                He takes it from her, pointing.

                What, what does this character mean?

SU-LING: I don't know.

MERCHANT LI: I see. Isn't your Poa-Poa going to teach you to read?

SU-LING: She doesn't know how.

MERCHANT LI: Of course not, but what about you?

SU-LING: Poa-Poa says girls don't need to read.

MERCHANT LI: *(Amused.)* My my! Goodness me! That's what she
                says is it? And here I thought, I hoped that times had
                changed! *(A beat, a decision.)* There's another saying,
                "The smallest revolution is still a step forward."
                Have you heard of this saying?

SU-LING: What does it mean?

MERCHANT LI: Ha-ha… Well. Come into my back room and I'll
                show you.

Scene 10 1913

                MERCHANT LI's back room.

MERCHANT LI: Stroke by stroke you have to put this into your
                memory. So that when you see this character,
                automatically you will think HORSE. HORSE.

SU-LING (11): *(Mimicking him.)* HORSE! HORSE!

MERCHANT LI: Concentrate.

SU-LING: HORSE! HORSE!

MERCHANT LI: I thought that you wanted to learn.

SU-LING: I do.

MERCHANT LI: Then let's see you do the strokes.

> *She sloppily writes the character.*

SU-LING: How about that?

MERCHANT LI: It's a bit messy.

SU-LING: Well, my horse, my horse is running.

MERCHANT LI: Oh is it? Where is it going?

SU-LING: It's running away. It has a long way to go, all the way back to its field, where it belongs.

MERCHANT LI: Oh I see. Hmmm. That's not what I see.

SU-LING: What? What do you see?

MERCHANT LI: The horse is in a hurry, but she is not going anywhere.

SU-LING: Then what is she doing?

MERCHANT LI: She's rushing, because she's impatient. And tired and maybe even lazy—

SU-LING: I am not!

MERCHANT LI: I thought we were talking about the horse.

SU-LING: Right.

MERCHANT LI: There might be some treats waiting for her.

SU-LING: Really? I think the horse likes sesame balls.

MERCHANT LI: I think that there might be sesame balls.

SU-LING: Uh-hmm.

MERCHANT LI: One more time, and make it a horse standing still.

SU-LING: Of course the horse has to stand still. She will be perfectly still! How else could she eat the sesame balls!

> *Picking up the brush she draws the character. Projected on her face and his, a series of Chinese characters that float and swirl.*

Scene 11 1914

> *The courtyard of Chen, POA-POA's employers. Upper class.*

POA-POA: You've taken so long again! What an embarrassing child you are! The other seamstresses had their meal already. Where were you?

> *SU-LING hands POA-POA's lunch of dumplings to her.*

SU-LING (12):   There's somebody over there, watching us.

POA-POA: Ignore them. Servant children.

SU-LING: It's a girl! And a boy. He's taking his shirt off…

POA-POA: The way these lousy servants raise their children! They should be working, not playing… And look at the size of her feet! Ridiculous!

SU-LING: I'm going to see what they're doing.

POA-POA: I forbid you to walk over there.

SU-LING: But Poa-Poa, they're playing a game!

POA-POA: What has gotten into you! No. They are the wrong sort of people!

Su-Ling (Marjorie Chan) and Merchant Li (John Ng)

Laughter from off stage. A shuttlecock (Chinese hacky-sac, made from old newspapers and feathers) comes flying on stage, almost hitting them. POA-POA holds SU-LING's arm stiffly and faces in the opposite direction of the children.

Here she comes. Just, just be quiet and ignore her and she'll go away.

MING, a dirty and dishevelled servant girl around the same age as Su-Ling runs on. Her feet are very loosely bound.

SU-LING: Hi.

POA-POA: Don't talk to her. She could have a disease!

MING: My apologies. Did it hit you?

SU-LING: Uhhhh...

POA-POA: Don't answer! Ignore her!

Without POA-POA seeing, SU-LING shakes her head "no". MING indicates silently "Where did it go?" SU-LING indicates with her head. The shuttlecock is very close to POA-POA.

Don't look at her! Are you looking at her?

SU-LING: No.

With her foot, SU-LING tries to push the shuttlecock away from POA-POA and towards MING.

POA-POA: We will just stand here. Like the good mannered ladies that we are. And we will have patience, until this ruffian goes away.

SU-LING gives up on moving the shuttlecock.

SU-LING: She's still here, Poa-Poa.

POA-POA: I know, I can smell her.

SU-LING: Maybe we should move?

POA-POA: This is the courtyard for the higher employees. I am sure she knows that. Unless she is thick. Does she look thick to you?

SU-LING: Why don't we have our food over there, on that other bench?

POA-POA: Yes, let's go. I can't stand her stare any longer.

Scene 12 1915

In MERCHANT LI's shop.

MERCHANT LI: Take a look at this!

He takes out a full 'English' tea set.

SU-LING (13):   What is it?

MERCHANT LI: Tea cups! Foreign tea cups from across the river! What do you think?

You would never have to hold a cup of tea that was too hot! Not with this handle and this plate underneath.

SU-LING: That's quite smart!

MERCHANT LI: Isn't it?

SU-LING: *(Admiring it.)* Umm-hmm.

MERCHANT LI: Cup of tea?

SU-LING: Please!

MERCHANT LI prepares the tea.

SU-LING: You know, you're much nicer than I thought you were.

MERCHANT LI: Excuse me?

SU-LING: Well, when I first met you, you were very rude.

MERCHANT LI: I was not. I was accommodating.

SU-LING: Oh maybe you don't remember. But I do. You were mean.

MERCHANT LI: I was mean.

SU-LING: And I didn't like you at all. You didn't seem to have any manners.

MERCHANT LI: You sound like your Poa-Poa.

SU-LING: No, Poa-Poa would say... *(Impersonating POA-POA.)* There are too many foreign devils in this city... Take care Ling-Ling! If you should see one, go the other way.

MERCHANT LI: She didn't say that!

SU-LING: Oh yes she did!

MERCHANT LI: What else does she say?

SU-LING: I don't know. She talks about when we lived in the village a lot.

MERCHANT LI: I guess she would.

SU-LING: Why did you leave the village?

> *She touches him on his arm, but he pulls away.*

MERCHANT LI: Your Poa-Poa didn't tell you?

SU-LING: No.

> *Beat.*

We left the village because we had nowhere to live. After my Ma-Ma and Ba-Ba died, my father's family didn't want us.

MERCHANT LI: My family didn't want me. They disowned me.

SU-LING: What did you do to make them so mad?

MERCHANT LI: Why do you assume I did something?

SU-LING: Did you?

MERCHANT LI: No. I failed to do something. To be a dutiful son.

SU-LING: That can be bad.

MERCHANT LI: I was engaged to be married. A good match. She had a round face, always smiling. But, could you imagine me, a farmer?

SU-LING: Why not?

MERCHANT LI: Breaking my back to grow enough wheat to pay the landlord! No, the call of the Republic was stronger! It was a young man's dream... I thought I could change China.

SU-LING: What happened to the round face farming girl?

MERCHANT LI: She married somebody else.

SU-LING: Did you love her?

MERCHANT LI: You ask very personal questions.

SU-LING: If you did, why did you leave her in the first place?

MERCHANT LI: Sometimes you have to make choices that are hard. That hurt.

SU-LING: Even if you end up alone?

MERCHANT LI: *(Harsh.)* Come on. Get on with your reading.

              He hands her a book.

SU-LING: The story of Yexian? Why? Everyone knows this story already.

MERCHANT LI: *(Snaps.)* But you haven't read it!

              He crosses over to his abacus, and starts doing figures.

Scene 13 1915

> *SU-LING starts as if reading to MERCHANT LI,*
> *eventually moving towards telling the story directly*
> *to the audience.*

SU-LING (13): Once, before the time of the emperors, there was a poor girl named Yexian.

Her mother had died, and so her father married again. The poor girl missed her own mother very much and would go down to the river every day to cry. She cried so much the river started to overflow. The river god took pity on her and sent a golden carp to cheer her up. Everyday, the golden carp would surface and pillow its head on the bank. One day the stepmother went down to the river and when the fish put its head on the bank, she killed it with a cleaver. Then she cooked it and buried the bones in a dunghill. The next day, Yexian went down to the river to see her friend, but the carp was gone. The river god again took pity on her. He said, "Do not cry. Your stepmother has killed the fish and buried the bones. Find the bones and hide them in your room. Whatever you shall want, pray to them and your wishes will be granted." And so she did.

One day Yexian heard about a festival in the village but her stepmother wouldn't allow her to go. Alone at home, Yexian prayed to the bones of the carp. She asked for a pair of shoes covered in glass beads and a dress to match. The carp granted her wishes and off she went to the festival! She was having a wonderful time when her stepmother spotted her. Afraid that she'd been caught, Yexian started running. She was running so fast that she left behind one of her shoes! The King came along and found it, shining in the night. He searched all over his land for the owner of the magnificent shoe. Until finally, the King came to Yexian's house. She put on the shoe

and it fit her perfectly. She had the smallest feet in
the land. And so, the King asked her to marry him.
And at last, the King and Yexian could be together.

Scene 14 1915

> *SU-LING is carrying POA-POA's meal and
> walking dreamily when she comes across MING
> playing with her hacky-sac.*

SU-LING (13):   That looks like fun.

MING: It is.

SU-LING: Where's your friend? I mean, the boy. The one you
                 were with.

MING: He's not my friend. He's my brother.

SU-LING: Oh.

MING: He's so stupid. He says he's going to join the army.

SU-LING: What's wrong with that?

MING: Who wants to follow all those rules?

SU-LING: Well, at least he's strong.

MING: How would you know?

SU-LING: Well, he looked strong.

MING: *(Playing her hacky-sac.)* Do you want to try?

SU-LING: No, uh, my grandmother. She wouldn't like it.

MING: Are you afraid of getting caught?

SU-LING: No.

MING: Where do you work?

SU-LING: I don't. Poa-Poa took this job… But we, we're not
                 really servants.

MING: She does servant work.

SU-LING: I know, but...

MING: So you don't have to work?

SU-LING: No.

MING: What do you do all day?

SU-LING: Nothing really.

MING: Nothing? You don't do anything?

SU-LING: No. Are you even supposed to be here?

MING: Where?

SU-LING: In this courtyard.

MING: I can go anywhere I want. The Chens practically treat me like family!

SU-LING: Do they?

MING: I can eat whatever I want...and...I don't work either! I sleep all day!

               Noticing something in the distance, SU-LING stops.

SU-LING: Oh no. I think it's him.

MING: Who?

SU-LING: Don't turn around. Master Chen is heading this way!

MING: What is he doing over here!

SU-LING: He's coming right for us!

MING: Oh no!

               MING turns and bows, but stops.

MING: Master Ch— Where is he?

SU-LING: (*Laughing.*) You thought he was actually coming!

MING: No, I didn't.

SU-LING: Yes you did. Admit it!

MING: I knew it was a trick.

SU-LING: Right!

> MING looks off in the other direction.

MING: Oh no. Master Chen is coming.

SU-LING: No, he's not!

MING: He is, he really is…

SU-LING: I'm not that stupid.

MING: Shut up! Look!

> SU-LING looks and spots Chen and his entourage.

SU-LING: Is that him? He's looks so old.

MING: I better go…

> MING exits hurriedly, with her head bowed.

SU-LING: Wait—what about me?

> POA-POA enters in a rush.

POA-POA: Su-Ling! What are you doing?

SU-LING: I was just—

POA-POA: Where is he now?

SU-LING: Master Chen?

POA-POA: Of course. Who else?

SU-LING: He's looking right at us!

POA-POA: Come here, hurry up. Sit still! For one second. And wipe that expression off your face! Pretend you are contemplating blossoms.

SU-LING: Why?

POA-POA: Just do as I tell you!

                They wait, still, contemplating blossoms.

POA-POA: I think he went down to the east courtyards. I just
                hope Master Chen didn't witness your little
                exchange with that servant girl! What were you two
                up to?

SU-LING: I was only talking.

POA-POA: You know better than to speak with her. This is not
                the street.

SU-LING: I don't know why it's such a big deal!

POA-POA: Your brain must be as small as your feet! We might
                be poor. We might have nothing but we still have
                our dignity. You should be a reflection of me. If you
                are not clean, if your clothes and hair aren't tidy, it
                speaks of me. He'll think that I am not responsible!
                Not responsible enough to clothe my own
                granddaughter! And because I have a fair wage,
                Master Chen might think "What does she do with
                the money I give her?" And maybe a servant, maybe
                even your little friend will make up a rumour. I am a
                drinker, I am a gambler. I steal opium from the
                household. And very soon, oh, it could happen quite
                quickly! I could lose my job. And then? We would be
                out on the street. Do you understand?

SU-LING: Yes, Poa-Poa.

POA-POA: It's time we thought more of your future. You must
                only associate with the right class or we will never
                find a proper husband for you. I have to invest in
                better clothing. I'll need to consult a matchmaker,
                you'll have to start sewing a pair of engagement
                shoes! Marriage is only around the corner.

Scene 15 1916

> *MERCHANT LI's shop. SU-LING discovers a book, old and greasy with an erotic drawing on the cover. Opening it, there is a flood of light and fabric. Erotic pen and ink drawings of men and women with bound feet are projected onto SU-LING's face and the surrounding fabrics. She flips through faster and faster, and the images come up faster and faster overlapping until, MERCHANT LI enters. She slams the book shut.*

MERCHANT LI: You shouldn't be looking at that.

SU-LING (14):   What is it?

MERCHANT LI: Just a book.

SU-LING: What is the man doing with the woman's foot?

MERCHANT LI: It doesn't concern you. It's for adults.

SU-LING: She had all her bindings off! In front of a man!

MERCHANT LI: This book is secret.

SU-LING: Why is it a secret?

MERCHANT LI: You can have this…this ribbon!

SU-LING: A ribbon?

MERCHANT LI: What about this comb? It's ivory.

SU-LING: I have a lot of hair. One comb won't hold it up.

MERCHANT LI: Fine fine, here's two of them. Just don't… Our secret, alright? Do we have a deal?

SU-LING: What about the ribbon?

> *He hands it to her.*

Scene 16 1917

> *SU-LING and POA-POA are in the market, looking at various booths.*

POA-POA: Ling-Ling, please, stand still for just one minute.

SU-LING (15):   Is that him? I think I've seen him before.

POA-POA: Don't point, you silly girl.

SU-LING: Where did he go?

POA-POA: Please, we're here to do our shopping.

SU-LING: *(Seeing him.)* Oh Poa-Poa. He's looking over here.

POA-POA: Now tell me, which peach is more ripe? This one or this one?

SU-LING: He's very handsome.

> *SU-LING gives a very small wave.*

POA-POA: Stop it.

SU-LING: He's waving back!

POA-POA: You'll ruin everything. You can't show too much interest.

SU-LING: I was only waving at him.

POA-POA: Only an indecent girl like you would be so brazen. His family probably saw that.

SU-LING: They're watching?

POA-POA: You're as dense as your mother! Continue shopping as if nothing is unusual!

SU-LING: But who is he?

POA-POA: That young man—don't look at him!—He is the youngest son of the Wong family.

SU-LING: They run a vegetable stand! I pass by there everyday before...before I bring you your meal.

POA-POA: They don't just run it. They own the farm where all those vegetables come from. A very prosperous farm. And they need a strong woman to help them run it. I've spent a lot of money on the matchmaker to arrange this day. Just act naturally. They only want to get a look at you, to see if you're strong enough.

SU-LING: Well, I'm pretty strong!

POA-POA: I know that. Stand up straight!

        SU-LING does so, but ridiculously.

What are you, a soldier? Just pretend they're not looking.

SU-LING: Where do you think the family is?

POA-POA: Probably in that tea shop.

SU-LING: *(Seeing them.)* Ooooh!

POA-POA: Don't look at them!

SU-LING: Poa-Poa... They don't look very happy.

POA-POA: I know. Take that sack of rice.

SU-LING: The whole thing?

POA-POA: Listen to your grandmother!

        POA-POA dumps the sack of rice onto SU-LING.

SU-LING: Oooomph! But Poa-Poa—

POA-POA: Do you want to be married or not?

SU-LING: To him?

POA-POA: Well not to the donkey! Let's walk quickly. Come on! We'll show them how strong you are.

> POA-POA *rushes off, with SU-LING close behind*
> *struggling with the sack of rice.*

Scene 17 1917

> *The sound of abacus in the next room. SU-LING is*
> *reading a book half-heartedly in MERCHANT LI's*
> *back room. Spotting an embroidered jade-green dress,*
> *SU-LING sets down her book, and tries it on.*
> *MERCHANT LI enters.*

SU-LING (15): I, I only wanted to look at it...

MERCHANT LI: And then try it on?

SU-LING: Well, it looked like it would fit me...

MERCHANT LI: It might except that it's fastened incorrectly. You didn't notice that.

SU-LING: No.

MERCHANT LI: Here, let me fix it.

> *He starts to fasten it, but she pulls away.*

SU-LING: I can do it.

MERCHANT LI: Well, at least I get a chance to see what it will look like...I could just tweak the sleeve a little bit. Just don't let Young Miss Tang catch you in her clothes!

SU-LING: Is this for an engagement?

MERCHANT LI: No, for a festival in her village. She did all the embroidery herself!

SU-LING: I'd never have the patience to do that!

MERCHANT LI: And you should see her shoes, green silk. And tiny. Tinier than even your feet—

SU-LING: Mine?

MERCHANT LI: (*Over SU-LING.*) —And embroidered with flowers, astonishing workmanship! Glass actually sewn and cut into the shape of petals.

SU-LING: I really doubt that her feet could be smaller than mine.

MERCHANT LI: An exquisite shoe for an exquisite lady.

SU-LING: She wouldn't have worn her fancy shoes to your stinky shop.

MERCHANT LI: She didn't wear them to my shop. But she did bring them in. So that I could match the fabric for her dress.

SU-LING swishes about.

Which I think you've had on long enough.

He gestures for her to take off the dress, but SU-LING ignores him and keeps it on.

SU-LING: She's pretty then?

MERCHANT LI: Well, yes. As pretty as her family's money can buy.

SU-LING: Prettier than me?

MERCHANT LI: Well…

SU-LING: Smarter than me?

She prances about the shop.

SU-LING: (*High squeaky voice.*) Look at me, I'm little Miss Tang. I have tiny tiny feet. That's why I'm stupid, stupid because they bound my feet and all my brains got squeezed out. Ohhh-hooo hooo. Look at me!

MERCHANT LI: Her voice sounds nothing like that! Nobody's voice is that high!

SU-LING: (*Too low a voice.*) Look at me. I'm Miss Tang. I sound like a man! I look like a man too, except for my feet!

MERCHANT LI: That's not funny.

SU-LING: So why are you smiling? Does she really sound like a man?

MERCHANT LI: You should probably take that off now.

SU-LING: No, no, no, no. What were you going to say?

MERCHANT LI: Miss Tang might be pretty, but she's not particularly....bright.

SU-LING: I knew it! *(As Miss Tang.)* I'm going back to my village and at the festival everyone will want to dance with me! Ohh hooo hooo!

> *She embraces MERCHANT LI rather intimately and begins whirling wildly around the room.*

MERCHANT LI: Stop it...stop it! This isn't proper...

SU-LING: Oooh-hoo-hoo!

MERCHANT LI: I mean it! Stop it!

> *They crash into the counter sending fabric flying, spilling an inkwell, tearing the dress etc.*

MERCHANT LI: You idiot child!

SU-LING: My ankle...

MERCHANT LI: Take it off.

> *She does so in silence.*

SU-LING: I think I hurt myself.

MERCHANT LI: You ruined the dress!

SU-LING: Can I help you?

MERCHANT LI: I can't afford your kind of help.

SU-LING: What about a book? I didn't even get to—

MERCHANT LI: Just go.

SU-LING: Could I come back—

MERCHANT LI: NO! GET OUT!

Scene 18 1918

POA-POA praying.

POA-POA: Kwanyin. Goddess of compassion.

I look into Su-Ling's face and I can see her mother's face. They have the same frown. My poor Hua-Ling. Before my daughter's engagement, I had dreams. Dreams of fields filled with flowers, filled with poppies, and my daughter standing alone. But as Su-Ling's engagement presentation draws near... I haven't had any. No dreams, not of Su-Ling, not any at all.

Send me a dream, Kwanyin, so that I might see. Am I destined to make the same mistakes? Will this family have to eat the seeds of bitterness yet again?

Scene 19 1918

Shanghai apartment. SU-LING is reading when POA-POA enters. She quickly hides the book.

POA-POA: Where are your engagement shoes? The presentation meeting is next week.

SU-LING (16):   They're not ready!

POA-POA: But the Wong family needs to judge your handiwork!

SU-LING: I'm not finished! And I do want them to be perfect. To be a proud representation of our family.

POA-POA: Let me see them.

SU-LING: I haven't, haven't finished the embroidery.

POA-POA: I know that you are nervous! What young woman wouldn't be with the possibility of marriage! Let's see what you've done!

SU-LING: No, I can't.

POA-POA: Su-Ling. You don't have to worry. Though there are some that may have doubted us, I know that our fortunes will change. Last night, Kwanyin sent me a dream. It was so clear! Clear as day! Do you want to know what I saw?

SU-LING: No.

POA-POA: Plastered walls, Ling-Ling! Plastered walls! It means that in the new year we will live again in a prosperous household! One that will plaster all of their walls, and not just the outside. And when we go to the Wong House, carrying your magnificent lotus shoes, I'm sure I'll be right.

SU-LING: Right...is there any more gold thread?

POA-POA: What happened to the whole spool I gave you?

SU-LING: I've used it up...

POA-POA: How? It should have been enough for an entire dress!

SU-LING: I'm doing something...special.

POA-POA: Like what?

SU-LING: I was thinking of sewing open-ladders on the shoes.

POA-POA: It's a very intricate design, very difficult to do well. Are you sure you can handle it?

SU-LING: Of course, Poa-Poa. But it will take more time. Can't you delay the meeting with the Wongs?

POA-POA: They are anxious to get this transaction over with! We meet with them next week!

Scene 20 1918

MERCHANT LI's shop. MERCHANT LI crosses to where SU-LING usually sits, looking at Miss Tang's dress, now repaired. He opens a curtain to reveal rows of worn lotus shoes. He selects a pair, the tiniest. He places them under the gown, and softy caresses the green silk. SU-LING enters.

SU-LING (16): I need more gold thread.

MERCHANT LI: How very nice to see you too.

(Beat.) Is that all that you would like?

SU-LING: Yes.

MERCHANT LI: Not interested in anything else?

SU-LING: No.

MERCHANT LI: Aren't you bored without anything to read?

SU-LING: I said I'm here for gold thread!

MERCHANT LI: Fine. What kind of gold thread would you like?

SU-LING: I don't really know.

MERCHANT LI: What kind of embroidery are you doing? Tight small stitches, or swirling full ones? Or?

SU-LING: I, I don't know.

MERCHANT LI: Well, what is it that you are sewing?

SU-LING pulls out her lotus shoes that she has been sewing. They look dreadful.

MERCHANT LI: *(Laughing.)* You foolish girl! Those...those ratty little bags of cloth! What are those!

SU-LING: They're my engagement shoes!

MERCHANT LI: These are your engagement shoes! They wouldn't even get you engaged to a duck!

SU-LING: Don't laugh! I've been working very hard.

MERCHANT LI: Yes, yes be careful with your beautiful lotus shoes. I will honour them, cherish them!

               He bows to them mockingly.

SU-LING: Stop it, stop it.

MERCHANT LI: What have you done, you silly girl?

               She can no longer hold it in, and joins in the laughter.

SU-LING: They are terrible, aren't they?

MERCHANT LI: Oh little Su-Ling. I have clothed many a fine woman. So many different kinds of lotus shoes and never in my whole career have I ever seen such a disastrous pair!

SU-LING: *(Lightly.)* I know. I can't sew. Help me!

MERCHANT LI: What would you have me do?

SU-LING: Can't you repair them or something?

MERCHANT LI: They, my dear, are too far gone. Besides, women are supposed to make their own engagement shoes!

SU-LING: Please. Our meeting with the Wongs is tomorrow.

MERCHANT LI: Let me see your feet.

               MERCHANT LI very gently slips off SU-LING's everyday shoes.

SU-LING: Will you do it?

MERCHANT LI: I have to see. I'll just measure your, your feet now.

               He does so, in uncomfortable silence.

SU-LING: Have you finished?

MERCHANT LI: No. I need to, just a little more… Your feet, so tiny, just like Yexian's. And your shoe, your little tiny shoe. At the festival…

SU-LING: I leave it behind.

MERCHANT LI: Yes. I find the shoe and then I find you.

Scene 21 1918

> *A rhythm template only. Repeat and improvise within this structure as needed.*

POA-POA: Cut the pattern.

Select the fabric.

POA-POA/SL: Trace the designs.

Embroider the images.

MERCHANT LI/
POA-POA/S-L: Attach the lining.

MERCHANT LI/
SU-LING: Finish the top border.

Join the pieces at the toe and heel.

MERCHANT LI: Build the sole.

Stitch them together.

A lotus shoe.

> *The 'perfect pair' fall from the rafters and remain suspended.*

Scene 22 1918

> *The apartment. After the meeting.*

POA-POA: I can't believe it. Even though you behaved terribly...I think the Wongs were impressed!

SU-LING (16):   He had a very nice smile, didn't he?

POA-POA: I didn't notice. Luckily you kept your mouth shut.
              And your shoes kept them distracted. They didn't
              have time to pry too deeply into our family's history.

SU-LING: So the shoes? They were alright?

POA-POA: Didn't you see his mother? She spent the whole
              meeting examining your embroidery.

SU-LING: She didn't say anything.

POA-POA: That means she liked it! She couldn't find anything
              to criticize. But I thought you were going to sew
              open-ladders?

SU-LING: I changed my mind.

POA-POA: That's too bad.

SU-LING: I thought they might be too flashy. I didn't want to
              seem frivolous.

POA-POA: An open ladder would have been very impressive
              indeed! Though I suppose a classical style is better
              for an engagement pair.

SU-LING: So you think they'll say yes?

POA-POA: Now it isn't for sure, not yet. Though judging by
              your handiwork...

SU-LING: I'm going to get married!

POA-POA: And don't worry about the open ladders, we'll save
              the extra details for the wedding shoes!

              *POA-POA exits leaving SU-LING alone. She slips
              out a book from her hiding spot.*

SU-LING: (*Reading.*)

              The sun is rising in our China!

              The end of winter, the end of rain, the end of clouds!

              Together, the new couple look to the horizon!

The sun is rising! A happy couple start anew!

The sun will shine in the East!

Draw back the curtain! Let in the light!

The wedding chamber is filled with guests!

Here to feast and toast the new family!

The sun will shine in the West!

These two, the heaven-matched pair!

A pair as much as life and death and left and right!

Together, they will walk 'til their hair is white!

The sun will shine in the South!

Bow for the bride who will produce an heir!

Give birth to a new China! Give birth to a noble son!

Give birth to future princes and presidents!

The sun will shine in the North!

Happy heaven shines her light on this wedding day!

The joyous Earth proclaims in delight!

Dreams of a family and a couple come true!

Glorious are the faces of the happy family!

Their faces lit by the dawn of a new life!

Salutations to you, bride and bridegroom!

Glorious is this day!

Scene 23 1918

> *MERCHANT LI's shop. Subdued, SU-LING hands him a bundle of books.*

MERCHANT LI: You're getting faster and faster. How am I supposed to keep up?

SU-LING: I didn't finish them.

MERCHANT LI: You don't like butterfly poetry? I thought a girl your age would love the romance...

SU-LING: I don't want any more books. They're full of lies.

MERCHANT LI: They're just stories!

SU-LING: But all the stories end happily.

MERCHANT LI: And you don't like happy endings?

SU-LING: It is not as if I don't like them... I just don't believe in them anymore.

> *She is overcome with emotion.*

MERCHANT LI: What happened?

SU-LING: The Wongs said no.

MERCHANT LI: I see.

SU-LING: Because of my family. Because of the way my parents died.

MERCHANT LI: Yes. Well. Now, maybe...maybe there will be someone else. Who doesn't think that way. Who can see you, and not your past.

SU-LING: We spent all that we had on the matchmaker. Poa-Poa's had to go back to sewing for the Chens.

MERCHANT LI: I'm sure she's thrilled about that.

> *SU-LING smiles wanly, but does not laugh.*

MERCHANT LI: How about some tea?

SU-LING: No.

MERCHANT LI: Sesame balls? You love those.

SU-LING: Tea and sesame balls aren't going to make me feel better.

Beat.

MERCHANT LI: You know not all books are full of lies.

SU-LING: All the books I've read. All the books you own.

MERCHANT LI: What about the newspaper?

SU-LING: And read about the "Great War"?

MERCHANT LI: But things are changing, now that China has officially entered.

SU-LING: We have enough of our own problems. We're headed for war ourselves!

MERCHANT LI: Sounds like you already have been reading the paper.

SU-LING: What does a war in Europe have to do with us?

MERCHANT LI: I don't know. There's more out there than you think.

SU-LING: And here I thought I could experience the entire world in your back room, honourable Merchant Li.

MERCHANT LI: Perhaps you'll want to visit these places, or live there. It is legal for a woman to emigrate now.

SU-LING: Is it?

MERCHANT LI: Yes.

SU-LING: But a woman's not allowed to travel alone, is she?

MERCHANT LI: No.

SU-LING: Then what's the point?

Beat.

MERCHANT LI: I have heard about something new. It's very secret. It has only been translated recently. I could ask around…see if I can find it for you.

SU-LING: What is it?

MERCHANT LI: *A Doll's House.*

SU-LING: Sounds like a story for children.

MERCHANT LI: No. It's not a novel, it's a play. From Europe. It's very popular. I've heard the ladies at the teahouses talk about it. I'm sure that, that one of the actresses, she would know where to find it.

SU-LING: And why would the whores of Shanghai be reading this?

MERCHANT LI: It's about a young woman who discovers her own worth and walks away from her life.

SU-LING: That's just another story. No one could do that.

MERCHANT LI: Ah. Perhaps I have something else that might appease your appetite.

> *He goes to the cupboard and takes out a handful of dusty books which are not professionally bound.*

I haven't looked at them for quite some time. When I was more…political. You'll find some writings in there from a young woman, Qui-Jin. She tired of being the wife of a merchant's son and so she fled to Japan. But she returned to start a journal for women. People didn't like what Qui-Jin had to say. She didn't care. Less than a year later, she was beheaded by order of the Empress Dowager. She never even saw the Republic we were fighting for.

SU-LING: You knew her?

MERCHANT LI: A word of warning. The tides are ever-changing. The side you take today may be the wrong one tomorrow. I know that you are careful. But especially with these...these are special to me...it would not do to be found with them.

> *SU-LING takes the package and as she opens them, the characters are once again projected onto her face, though with a less gentle quality and more intensity. Light from behind like fire, creating a silhouette of SU-LING as if surrounded by flame.*

Scene 24 1918

> *The apartment.*

POA-POA: They saw you in their courtyard and thought you would make a suitable wife.

SU-LING: What?

POA-POA: I found someone else. The Chens. We move to their compound very soon. They were willing to overlook your past and have found a place in their household. They were particularly impressed with the size of your feet.

SU-LING: Poa-Poa—

POA-POA: You will marry Second Son Chen. Since they are so prosperous, you will not have to work for them. But, they did mention they prefer a girl who isn't intellectual. I told them you were not. They asked if you can read. I told them you do not. You do not read, do you?

SU-LING: No. Where would I have learned to read?

POA-POA: Good. Then we don't need to pack those books you've hidden!

> *POA-POA reveals the political books, and begins throwing them at SU-LING.*

POA-POA: And think, there was a time when I prayed to

Kwanyin every night, thanking her for such a dutiful granddaughter! You lying worm! Where did you get these from? Tell me! Did you steal them?

SU-LING: No, I found them.

POA-POA: Where?

SU-LING: By a rubbish heap...near the market.

POA-POA: What are they? What do they say?

SU-LING: Poa-Poa. They're nothing, just children's stories.

POA-POA: I don't believe you.

SU-LING picks up one of the books.

SU-LING: Look! "Once, before the time of the emperors—"

POA-POA grabs the book from her.

POA-POA: Enough! Who is filling your head with these ideas? Who taught you?

SU-LING: I taught myself.

POA-POA: Impossible. You're too stupid. Who is helping you?

POA-POA throws a book at SU-LING.

SU-LING: Poa-Poa! Stop! Stop!

POA-POA: Who is it?

SU-LING: Merchant Li...

POA-POA: It was him?

SU-LING: No! No... But... Near his shop...the school... even you have heard the boys' voices...and—and—they would do their lessons...and I could hear them.

POA-POA: You stupid girl. You are supposed to be a lady. Not some street ruffian hanging around school walls! I am in charge of your education. Are you listening to me now?

SU-LING: Yes, Poa-Poa.

POA-POA: Our family can regain some honour with this marriage.

SU-LING: I know.

                    Beat.

POA-POA: You will make a very good concubine.

SU-LING: Concubine? But I thought I would be—

POA-POA: What? First Wife?

SU-LING: Couldn't we find—

POA-POA: Who could we find? Who would want to marry you? You're getting old! You're already 16! I was married at 14! Master Chen needs a son. We need food and shelter. Be grateful for this arrangement.

SU-LING: I don't want to marry him.

POA-POA: Second Wife is not so bad.

SU-LING: I don't even know him!

POA-POA: You'll get to know him!

SU-LING: I won't marry him!

POA-POA: You want to live this way forever. Poor as a rat looking for that last grain of rice. You'll end up like your mother, dead or worse.

SU-LING: Why do you hate you own daughter?

POA-POA: You are a stupid and foolish girl! You are determined to ruin this family, the way your Ma-Ma has ruined us!

SU-LING: Is it because your mother left you?

POA-POA: What?

SU-LING: Your Ma-Ma didn't want to be a concubine either. That's why she ran away, isn't it? She hated her life!

POA-POA: That's not true!

SU-LING: She ran away and left you with your father and all his other wives!

POA-POA: Stop this!

SU-LING: What did she do? Where could she go? To the teahouses of Blood Alley! To become a whore!

POA-POA: No!

SU-LING: And at least you had something! At least you had a letter from her!

POA-POA: My Ma-Ma...

SU-LING: But you didn't read it!

POA-POA: *(Defeated.)* Oh Ling-Ling... Can't you see? I, I wish I had her letter, I wish I knew what it said...I can't even remember her face. My Ma-Ma... I burnt her, I burnt her letter...and now I'll never know...

SU-LING: Poa-Poa...

POA-POA: I was so stubborn!

SU-LING: You were young...

POA-POA: No. I was stubborn! My Ma-Ma...she called my father to the teahouse...she wanted to see me because she was dying...she begged me to come...but I couldn't. I was too proud and too ashamed of her...and she got more and more ill...

SU-LING: Didn't you want to see her?

POA-POA: I was too angry, and I let her die alone. Oh Su-Ling...

         SU-LING watches as POA-POA cries.

SU-LING: Poa-Poa. I'm sorry.

POA-POA: (*Pulling herself together.*) But...I burnt her letter so
            that I could better see the future. Don't you see, Su-
            Ling, the past only holds us back! To survive, you
            must let it go... We must choose a new path, a new
            direction! We cannot let history dictate our fate.

SU-LING: No.

            Crackling of the fire, as POA-POA opens the stove.

SU-LING: What are you doing?

POA-POA: Get your books! Bring them to the fire.

SU-LING: Please...

POA-POA: The pain of this family must end.

SU-LING: Poa-Poa...

POA-POA: You can end it.

            No response.

            You will marry Chen.

SU-LING: Honourable grandmother. I am grateful for this
            arrangement.

            *She bows low. Over the fire, SU-LING is holding the
            political books. They watch them burn, the light
            reflecting off of their faces as lights fade.*

            End of Act I.

Su-Ling (Marjorie Chan)

Act II

This act takes place September–November 1918. SU-LING is 16.

Scene 1

> *At his shop, MERCHANT LI reads "A Doll's House" distractedly, waiting for SU-LING to arrive.*
>
> *SU-LING enters her room in the Chen compound. It has plastered walls. Lights fade on MERCHANT LI. POA-POA enters with her cane.*

SU-LING: This is mine? All of it?

POA-POA: Look at these plastered walls! Just like in my dream! Look!

SU-LING: I can see them.

POA-POA: The entire courtyard is for our use!

SU-LING: There isn't even a tree.

> *MING enters in a rush with baggage, tripping on the threshold.*

POA-POA: Well. *(Gesturing with her cane.)* Put them down.

> *MING does so but does not leave, unsure.*

POA-POA: You may go.

MING: No. I mean…I am to stay, and unpack.

POA-POA: You? Not likely!—

MING: I'm…her servant.

POA-POA: *(Over MING.)* —There must be some mistake.

MING: There are no other servants available.

POA-POA: You're no better than a scullery maid. There must be somebody else!

MING: No, none.

POA-POA: I'll see about that.

>   *POA-POA goes towards the door.*

MING: First Wife chose me herself.

>   *POA-POA blanches and stops.*

POA-POA: Then… indeed…you are in the right place.

SU-LING: What's the matter?

POA-POA: What's your name? Something common I recall.

MING: Ming.

POA-POA: You don't need to use it or even remember it. Let us have a look at you. Hmmmph. Not very strong. And your clothes! You have a small tear in your pants. Can't you sew?

MING: Yes.

POA-POA: Just yes? Nothing else?

MING: Yes ma'am?

POA-POA: You will address me by my proper title!

MING: Yes…ummm… Virtuous Grandmother of She who will become Honourable Second Wife to Master Second Son Chen.

POA-POA: That's better. This is Su-Ling. You will keep her clothes in better repair than your own. How do you address her?

MING: Uh… She who will become Honourable Second Wife to Master Second Son Chen?

POA-POA: Are you trying to be funny? Mistress will do.

MING: Mistress. I am honoured to serve the Second Lady of the House.

SU-LING: I'm not married yet.

POA-POA: You don't need to talk to her unless you're giving an order.

SU-LING: Sorry.

POA-POA: You don't need to apologize for being a better class. Just accept it for what it is. *(To MING.)* Unpack those bags.

> *MING continues to unpack. When finished, she stands and waits for instruction.*

You'll need new bedsheets.

SU-LING: Do I? Why?

POA-POA: Why not? *(Under her breath.)* It's not our money. We'll get silk ones!

SU-LING: I'm hungry.

POA-POA: She can fetch us something when she's done. Tell her what you want.

SU-LING: What should I ask for?

POA-POA: Roasted duck, or steamed fish, or fine mushrooms, anything you want!

SU-LING: And do we eat with the family?

POA-POA: No, no. Not in this House. You will not see Second Son Chen until the wedding day.

SU-LING: Surely I won't have to call him Second Son Chen?

POA-POA: *(To MING.)* We'll have some roasted duck with rice and a plate of pickled cabbage.

SU-LING: He's going to be my husband and I can barely remember what he looks like!

POA-POA: What does it matter what he looks like?

SU-LING: I remember he's not young. And I guess First Wife isn't either.

POA-POA: You shouldn't say such things.

SU-LING: You'd think that she would come greet the second wife! Maybe we should send a message.

POA-POA: No, no. That is not necessary. No, I do believe that First Wife is quite aware of our presence. *(To MING.)* What are you still doing standing there? Go get our food.

               MING exits.

POA-POA: Is she gone?

SU-LING: Yes. I think so.

POA-POA: Remember, her loyalty is to First Wife and the Chens.

SU-LING: What are you saying? She's spying on me?

POA-POA: You can't trust her not to tell.

SU-LING: I haven't done anything.

POA-POA: This house is a different world than you are used to. Be prepared for change. In the next few weeks, you'll likely be offered some opium.

SU-LING: I won't smoke it.

POA-POA: You misunderstand me. When you are offered a pipe, I suggest you indulge. It will make things easier, and the days will pass more quickly. But watch that it does not control you. You need to survive in this household. So by all means indulge, but stay alert!

SU-LING: I'd rather avoid it.

POA-POA: *(With awkwardness.)* There are times when you will be grateful for its effects. A concubine has a very different function than being first wife. Do you understand? I know that this is not what you wanted, but you will fulfill your duty. Am I making sense? First wives are not for pleasure. They are chosen for many reasons...for economic reasons...for political reasons...but not for pleasure. It is your duty to be a pleasure to Chen. On the night of your wedding, do you know what will be asked of you?

SU-LING: I, I think so.

POA-POA: It will be painful at first, but you must not cry out.

SU-LING: I won't.

POA-POA: Don't worry. I will clean you after he has left. *(pause)* And yes, of course you should not call him Second Son Chen. You will call him Master.

Scene 2

MING is doing SU-LING's hair.

SU-LING: It's been a while since I've seen you.

MING does not respond.

SU-LING: Ming?

MING: What would you like, Mistress?

SU-LING: Nothing...I just thought that, well, maybe we could...

MING: I am your servant.

SU-LING: Why are you pretending not to remember me? I
              know that you do.

MING: Perhaps you were dressed very differently.

SU-LING: We weren't so fortunate then.

MING: And now you live here.

SU-LING: Yes. Yes I do.

              MING continues with her hair in silence.

SU-LING: How's your brother? The soldier?

MING: He's dead.

              *MING inserts a hair ornament roughly as POA-
              POA enters.*

SU-LING: Oww!

POA-POA: Is something the matter?

SU-LING: No. No. Just talking.

POA-POA: Talking?

SU-LING: Instructing her, Poa-Poa.

POA-POA: That's good! Make sure she knows who's in charge.
              I wanted to ask you, do you think you'll try the open
              ladders up the front of the shoe this time?

SU-LING: What?

POA-POA: For your wedding shoes. The pair you sewed for the
              Wongs were fine, but you'll need something more
              spectacular for the Chens.

SU-LING: I haven't thought about it yet.

POA-POA: Well, start thinking! What kind of thread you want
              and what kind of design. The open ladder would be
              nice, or some other fashionable style. It means
              another visit to Merchant Li.

SU-LING: When are we going?

POA-POA: Su-Ling. You can't go! Think of your position. What would the Chens say!

SU-LING: I'll need fabric if I'm to sew my shoes!

POA-POA: Young women do not go traipsing about town before their wedding. You are to stay here.

SU-LING: In this room?

POA-POA: And the courtyard!

SU-LING: What if I want to take a walk?

POA-POA: It is not permitted.

SU-LING: I'm not allowed to go anywhere?

POA-POA: If you must, we can take a trip to Kwanyin's temple. There, you can ask for her compassion before your wedding.

SU-LING: Fine.

POA-POA: *(To MING.)* Go arrange some transport.

                MING throws SU-LING a look as she exits.

SU-LING: What's the hurry?

POA-POA: I might as well go to Merchant Li's as soon as I can! Won't he be in for a surprise?

                POA-POA exits leaving SU-LING alone.

Scene 3

                MERCHANT LI's shop. POA-POA is looking at fabrics.

MERCHANT LI: Wedding! But Master Wong— They told me that—

POA-POA: What did they tell you?

MERCHANT LI: Nothing. Only that—

POA-POA: The Wongs were not suitable. Really, the Wongs are only common merchants. Su-Ling will be the Honoured Second Wife of Second Son Chen.

MERCHANT LI: You mean third wife.

POA-POA: No, Second Wife. I don't like these ones. My granddaughter needs fabrics of the highest quality.

MERCHANT LI: Of course. But Chen, he had a wedding last winter, didn't he? For a new concubine.

POA-POA: You are mistaken. These silks are slightly better.

MERCHANT LI: But I remember you bought fabrics to sew wedding linens!

POA-POA: Your memory is failing you. That wedding was for one of the Chen cousins.

MERCHANT LI: Indeed.

                He turns away, lost in thought.

POA-POA: Merchant Li? Merchant Li. Show me that bolt over there.

MERCHANT LI: Of course.

POA-POA: It would be nice for her wedding dress.

MERCHANT LI: Is she, is Su-Ling looking forward to her wedding?

POA-POA: What young woman wouldn't be? A regular little bride, fluttering about like a lark, getting all her linens ready!

MERCHANT LI: And has she, has she started sewing her wedding shoes?

POA-POA: Merchant Li. You seem...distracted today. I'm wondering what could be bothering you.

                MERCHANT LI is silent.

POA-POA: This is a wonderful opportunity for Su-Ling, wouldn't you agree?

MERCHANT LI: Yes.

POA-POA: I wouldn't want anyone to ruin her chance at happiness.

MERCHANT LI: No.

POA-POA: The Chens are very powerful. I'm sure that you appreciate their business. Unless, you feel otherwise?

Beat.

MERCHANT LI: Do you see this fabric? Run your hands over it.

POA-POA: Very good. Soft. Surprising with so much embroidery.

MERCHANT LI: (Passive-agressively.) This type of stitching is done by women of the mountains... It seems very simple when you first see it, but look closely... See how each piece of thread carries through and hooks onto the next in a fish-scale pattern. That is what creates the softness and strength. Do you like it?

POA-POA: Yes I'll take this one too.

MERCHANT LI: I'll bring the fabrics that you chose, as well as some new designs. I'll bring them to the compound.

POA-POA: Of course there will be no charge for delivery.

MERCHANT LI: Only the very best for Master Chen. And this way, Su-Ling can have the opportunity to look at the fabrics as well. I'll have some things from Europe that she might like.

POA-POA: I doubt it. What would she do with European things?

Scene 4

> *SU-LING sitting with a wooden tray crowded with tiny ceramic dishes of succulent dumplings, pickled vegetables, onion cakes etc. Using expensive chopsticks, she picks at her food, while watching MING clean the floor.*

SU-LING: This is better than last night's meal. It was so greasy.

MING: My apologies.

SU-LING: And the pork had gone off. They should use fresh meat.

MING: My apologies.

SU-LING: Don't you say anything else?

MING: What would you like me to say?

SU-LING: Anything else!

MING: There has been a delivery from the market. Your wedding linens have arrived. Your honourable grandmother is waiting for you in the sitting room.

SU-LING: Wha— Why are you telling me this only now?

MING: I was waiting until you were finished eating.

SU-LING: Stupid! You should've told me earlier.

MING: My apologies.

> *SU-LING downs her teacup, hard.*

SU-LING: You might as well eat the rest!

MING: No thank you.

SU-LING: There's some dishes I haven't even touched!

MING: No thank you. I'm not hungry.

SU-LING: Take them back to your family!

MING: My mother prepared the meal. No thank you.

SU-LING: You pig-headed little servant! You should be so lucky to eat my scraps! I may only be a concubine, but I still deserve to be treated with respect!

MING: You don't know anything...do you?

SU-LING: I know what a proper servant is!

MING: Do you? Who takes care of your clothes? Who bathes your feet? Who brings you your food? My family has worked here for generations. If I wanted, my mother would only give you the bottom of the rice, brown and burnt. If I wanted, I would never use fresh water for your tea. If I wanted, the only meat you would get would be pig testicles. Every day. Maybe that's the only meat I've ever served you!

SU-LING: You...just...just...Go! Go tell my grandmother I'm coming!

                MING exits, perhaps not as fast as she should.

                You forgot to take away the dishes!

                Looking after MING, SU-LING carefully dissects her dumpling, peering inside it.

Scene 5

                Sitting room. MERCHANT LI and POA-POA are examining the trousseau linen. MING is helping to unfold the fabrics.

POA-POA: They're tremendous. Just like a dream.

                Enter SU-LING.

POA-POA: Where were you? We've been waiting.

MERCHANT LI: It is good to see you.

SU-LING: Do you always make deliveries?

POA-POA: With our status, comes service. Have a look before I take the fabrics over to Chen's seamstresses.

SU-LING: How many linens do I need?

POA-POA: For the bed, you need new undersheets, pillow covers, embroidered blankets and of course bed curtains, one set for the overhang, one for the bed proper. Then there's the linens for the room—

SU-LING: Yes, Poa-Poa. I just think... you ordered so much.

POA-POA: The Chen name is good for the credit!

MERCHANT LI: These ones are the highest quality silk.

POA-POA: Any chance of getting something from overseas? I don't mean that European junk. But I heard that Japanese silks...

MERCHANT LI: Shipments are difficult. With the war and all.

POA-POA: Japan is not that far is it? I'm willing to pay.

SU-LING: But Japan is not really on our side!

POA-POA: And what do you know about the war?

SU-LING: Nothing. Just that.

POA-POA looks at her suspiciously.

POA-POA: You've got more important things to worry about. Merchant Li, as skillful a trader as you are, do you think you could possibly acquire fabrics from Japan?

MERCHANT LI: Possibly.

POA-POA: Excellent! I wouldn't normally be interested in foreign things, but times change! Let's see the rest! We've barely enough time to get this wedding arranged!

SU-LING: There's more?

POA-POA: Those were just for your linens. These are the fabrics for your wedding dress.

> POA-POA *takes some red silk and drapes it on SU-LING.*

Isn't it everything that you ever hoped for?

> MERCHANT LI *moves to help, his attention on SU-LING rather than the fabric.*

MERCHANT LI: It's beautiful.

POA-POA: Well, what do you think? Do you want to get married in this?

SU-LING: Uh, yes. It's fine.

POA-POA: You don't like it? What's wrong with it?

> POA-POA *holds up another piece of fabric over SU-LING, smothering her.*

POA-POA: How about this one?

SU-LING: Stop that. Please. That's enough.

POA-POA: What's the matter with you?

SU-LING: It's a little warm…take it off…

POA-POA: Are you sick?

> SU-LING *bends over, faint.*

SU-LING: Stop. Just let me go!

> SU-LING *escapes for the fresh air of the courtyard.*

POA-POA: Su-Ling!

MERCHANT LI: Is she going to be alright?

POA-POA: She'll be fine. Probably just overexcited!

MERCHANT LI: I should be going as well. Good to do business with you.

POA-POA: Now, Merchant Li, if you do get anything new, that some of the other families buy, you'll tell me right away, won't you? Su-Ling must have the very best.

MERCHANT LI: She deserves as much.

POA-POA: (*Low.*) I know we've had our differences, but this is the beginning of both our fortunes! We should be grateful.

MERCHANT LI: Good day.

Scene 6

> *MERCHANT LI catches up with SU-LING in the courtyard.*

SU-LING: You shouldn't be here.

MERCHANT LI: I was here to make a delivery, that's all.

SU-LING: And you've done so. Goodbye.

MERCHANT LI: Did you enjoy them? The writings of Qui-Jin? Maybe we could read them together!

SU-LING: No. The books are gone. I burnt them.

MERCHANT LI: What?

SU-LING: The Chens prefer I don't read. And so I won't.

MERCHANT LI: But how could you stop?

SU-LING: I can't believe you had the nerve to come here. What do you want?

MERCHANT LI: I brought that book I was telling you about. The play. *A Doll's House.*

> *He takes out a package.*

SU-LING: I don't want it, I told you that.

MERCHANT LI: Take it. Please.

SU-LING: Put it away. You'll get me in trouble.

MERCHANT LI: The character, her name was Nora. You see, she was unhappy...So she leaves. A little like Qui-Jin.

SU-LING: I can't be seen with you. Don't you understand?

MERCHANT LI: Read it...and, and tell me what you think.

SU-LING: Stop this! You have to leave!

MERCHANT LI: Take it, then I'll go. It's, it's a gift. From me, take it!

She takes the book.

SU-LING: Now get out of here! Go!

MERCHANT LI: Wait, I think you should know—

SU-LING: No, I never want to see you again—

MERCHANT LI: I don't want you to be scared, but Chen—

SU-LING: Get out!

MERCHANT LI: I heard something about him—

SU-LING: Go! And don't come back!

MERCHANT LI exits. MING emerges from around the corner. Beat.

SU-LING: My grandmother doesn't need you?

MING: No, Mistress.

SU-LING: Well, then. Good. You can do the rest of my room next.

SU-LING starts to go.

MING: There was this concubine. She was just like you.

SU-LING: What?

MING: She started having an affair. With a young soldier who used to be a servant on the grounds. They'd meet in her courtyard, or sometimes by the pigpen or the washing room. The soldier was in love, but the concubine was careless, and First Wife caught them. Of course she told her husband. And of course he was furious. He tied the concubine to the hitch posts by the stables, where the servants could see. He stuffed her mouth with dirty rags. She could hardly breathe. Then, he poured raw alcohol onto the rag. She started to choke. She was suffocating and drowning at the same time. But that took too long, so he set the rag on fire. It still took too long.

SU-LING: You're lying...

MING: Then why are there burn marks by the stables?

SU-LING buckles and MING catches her.

Scene 7

That evening. SU-LING's room. Ming is setting up the water and basin, when POA-POA rushes in, also carrying a basin.

POA-POA: You can stop what you're doing.

SU-LING: What's going on?

POA-POA: I thought that today, perhaps I would wash my granddaughter's feet.

SU-LING: It's not necessary.

POA-POA: Come, Ling-Ling, let me wash your feet. I'll wash them just like you were a little girl again. I'd hold you while you cried. You don't cry any more though do you?

SU-LING: No.

POA-POA: You were so little. It hurt. It was hard, but you were happy weren't you? You're happy now aren't you?

SU-LING: Poa-Poa...what is Chen like?

POA-POA: Oh, Master Chen is a very nice man, with quite a sense of humour. You shouldn't worry at all. He chose you himself. He's bound to like you!

SU-LING: I just don't know him.

POA-POA: Well, what more do you need to know? Because you should ask me, Su-Ling. There will always be those that are jealous. They're simply out to make trouble. Don't mind their whispering and their gossip.

SU-LING: Then tell me more about Chen!

POA-POA: *(To MING.)* Here, get out of the way. Don't you have ears? I said, I'll clean my granddaughter's feet! Go on, get out.

> *POA-POA pushes MING roughly out of the way.*

SU-LING: Poa-Poa what are you doing!

POA-POA: You need a proper washing. She doesn't do it properly! Does she get into the toes and into the crevice? It's very important, you know!

SU-LING: Just stop this! Let the girl do it!

POA-POA: What?

SU-LING: Go back to your room!

POA-POA: I'm just trying to help!

SU-LING: I don't need your help!

POA-POA: I'm your grandmother!

SU-LING: Just go! Leave me alone!

POA-POA: Fine. Be alone! I'll just stay in my room until I die!

POA-POA sets her basin down hard and exits.

SU-LING: Poa-Poa!

MING starts cleaning SU-LING's feet.

MING: You ask too many questions. Someone's going to get hurt.

SU-LING: It has nothing to do with you!

MING: Remember my brother?

SU-LING: He died...

MING: He died a few days after the concubine.

SU-LING: What?

MING: The Chens told our family he shot himself. With his own gun.

SU-LING: He was the soldier?

MING: He was still in training. Where would he get a gun?

Scene 8

Each character onstage in their own reality.

MERCHANT LI in an opium den.

MERCHANT LI: No, not tea this time. Bring me a pipe, and a girl.

POA-POA is alone in her room, praying fervently..

POA-POA: Kwanyin, Goddess of compassion. Save me from my dream. I saw Ma-Ma walking away...her lonely footprints in the snow, and blood...

MING, crying, in the washing room. She is furiously wringing out wet clothes.

MING: Someone's going to get hurt...someone's going to get hurt!

SU-LING, in her room, pulls out "A Doll's House".
As she begins to read, text, both Norwegian words
and Chinese characters begin to float across her face.

SU-LING: (*Reading.*) Try to becalm, and bring peace to your thoughts, my frightened little songbird. You can rest secure. I have wide wings to shelter you. Here you are safe; here I can protect you, like a hunted dove I've saved from the claws of the hawk. Soon, I'll calm your poor beating heart. Believe me Nora, it will be alright. Tomorrow all this will seem quite different; then everything will be as before...

    MERCHANT LI laughing, is drinking from a tiny lotus shoe, spilling alcohol onto his face. Lights fade and his laughter continues.

Scene 9

    SU-LING's room.

MING: Mistress. Your grandmother would like to see the shoes.

SU-LING: Is she coming here now?

MING: She's waiting in her room.

SU-LING: I'm not finished yet.

MING: The wedding is next week.

SU-LING: I know. Don't you think I know that!

    She pretends to sew for a bit.

SU-LING: Oh! Stupid! I just broke a needle!

MING: There's another package.

SU-LING: No. They're all broken.

MING: How can they all be broken.

SU-LING: Because they are.

MING: Are you sure?

SU-LING: Why would I lie? Go to the seamstresses and get me
                   some more! Go!

MING: Yes Mistress.

                   *MING exits. Setting aside her sewing, SU-LING
                   reaches into her bedding for a package of needles.
                   Methodically she snaps them one by one.*

Scene 10

                   *MERCHANT LI's shop. He has recently returned
                   from the tea-house/opium den.*

MERCHANT LI: Ah. Pretty Su-Ling. The great Empress returns. And
                   how is it that she graces our presence?

SU-LING: I sent my servant for some needles.

MERCHANT LI: I thought that you never wanted to see me again?
                   And yet here you are.

SU-LING: I read the play.

MERCHANT LI: What did you think?

SU-LING: It seemed very cold of her to just leave her family
                   and responsibility like that.

MERCHANT LI: She's trapped.

SU-LING: She could have killed herself.

MERCHANT LI: That's for cowards.

SU-LING: Or for those with no other escape.

MERCHANT LI: She is a survivor. She has her freedom in the end.

SU-LING: So Nora walks out the door? What happens to her
                   after the door closes? Is she like Qui-Jin,
                   leaving...only to find death?

MERCHANT LI: Tell me, what do you think is the reason for Nora leaving?

SU-LING: Well, she feels that...if only he had said... I don't know. There is nothing for her. How is she to survive?

MERCHANT LI: Why is that so important? What's important is that she leaves!

SU-LING: She ran away, but did she have something to run to...?

He doesn't answer.

SU-LING: If Chen or First Wife ever found out that I came here... Why did you want me to read this?

MERCHANT LI: I only wanted to—I thought that you would enjoy it.

SU-LING: And that's all?

MERCHANT LI: Why else?

They are close.

SU-LING: You smell...you smell like...my father. After a night spent in an opium den.

MERCHANT LI: Didn't you ever wonder how a lowly merchant like myself has managed to survive through all the changes of the guard? Su-Ling, I'd do anything for you.

SU-LING: You would?

MERCHANT LI: Of course. Remember your engagement shoes? Remember how small they were? How I took your feet in my hands? Oh, if I could, if I could smell them again...Do you need help with your wedding shoes? I can help you.

He reaches for her.

SU-LING: No. Take your book. I have to go back.

Scene 11

MING is washing SU-LING's feet.

MING: I brought back needles. But I couldn't find you. Mistress.

SU-LING: Just wash my feet. They feel dirty.

Silence.

MING: Where did you go?

SU-LING: Where could I go? I was in Poa-Poa's room. Talking about the wedding.

MING: I looked in there. She was alone, just staring at the walls.

SU-LING: You must've missed me.

MING: What are you doing?

SU-LING: Having my feet washed.

MING: What about your wedding shoes?

SU-LING: I know.

MING: You've hardly begun.

SU-LING: I'll do something about them. I will. Soon.

MING suddenly stops washing.

SU-LING: Why are you stopping? What is it?

MING holds up a broken toe.

MING: Mistress, it…it…

SU-LING: What have you done?

MING: I was cleaning your toes and…

SU-LING: What?

MING: It was…rotten. It fell off.

SU-LING: Which one is it?

MING: Your baby toe…

> *SU-LING laughs ruefully.*

MING: It's not funny.

SU-LING: My Ma-Ma. She told me that we grew from seeds. And so I thought we grew from our baby toes.

MING: What should I do with it?

SU-LING: Throw it out.

MING: Don't you want it? You should be buried with it.

SU-LING: It doesn't matter any more. Just wash my feet. Please.

Scene 12

> *On one side of the stage, POA-POA and Ming prepare SU-LING's wedding garments. Simultaneously, SU-LING is at MERCHANT LI's on the other side of the stage.*

POA-POA: Help me with her wedding clothes. I want her to try them on.

MING: Yes, Honourable Mistress.

POA-POA: Even you can appreciate their beauty?

MING: Yes, of course.

SU-LING: I don't remember my father very much. Only his smell, like yours, too sweet. It would stick to you, all around. That must be what it's like.

MERCHANT LI: Where does Poa-Poa think you are this time?

MING: (*To POA-POA.*) At the temple of Kwanyin.

POA-POA: *(To MING.)* Really? Good!

SU-LING: I'm obviously devout.

MERCHANT LI: I knew that you would come back. I knew it.

SU-LING: Did you mean it? When you said you'd do anything
               for me?

MERCHANT LI: Anything.

·   *POA-POA and MING finish hanging the wedding
                   outfit. It should be hanging the same way that SU-
                   LING's mother is discovered.*

POA-POA: Now all that we need, are the wedding shoes to go
               with it!

SU-LING: I can't sew them. I tried.

MERCHANT LI: The wedding is next week?

SU-LING: Yes.

MING: She's, she's almost finished.

POA-POA: What's taking her so long?

                   *MING and POA-POA recede but are still present in
                   the scene.*

MERCHANT LI: The lotus shoe is a very complex creation. How the
               toe comes to such a point... How the arch curves just
               so...

SU-LING: Will you do it for me?

MERCHANT LI: When I see you walking. Walking with your golden
               lotus limp, forcing the muscles of your legs and hips
               to tighten. When I see you walking like that, I want
               to have you. I want to see all of you. Your feet,
               naked, and bare. The crevice in your foot, so tight.
               That is what I want.

                   *Stylized, MERCHANT LI slowly takes off her
                   slippers, and unwinds the leggings until the feet are*

bare. He caresses them, and dropping his pants, eventually penetrates both feet in turn. All the while, SU-LING speaks to him.

SU-LING: The, the shoes will have to be red of course...in silk. And, the open-ladder...for the front of the shoe. I, I want that. I would like that. I want carps on the side. They should be leaping. And, and the soles...put put a lotus bud, small and closed and tight. The rest...just fill it with prayers and wishes. Fill it with embroidery, so I can't see the shoe anymore. So that I can't see...

He finishes.

MERCHANT LI: Thank you. Thank you.

SU-LING extricates herself and stands before him like a doll. In his fantasy world, he dresses her until she is swaddled and drowning.

I will make the finest shoe for you. The finest. That is my promise.

MERCHANT LI exits.

SU-LING experiences severe abdominal cramps until finally she throws up with great difficulty a tiny pair of lotus shoes which she holds in her hands.

POA-POA and MING finish dressing SU-LING. It is now a few days later.

MING: Perfect!

POA-POA: What a fantastic pair of lotus shoes! I thought that perhaps you could not do it. Give them to me.

MING helps SU-LING with her balance as POA-POA puts the finishing touch on her doll.

What a beautiful bride you'll make tomorrow! And your feet! Still the same size as when you were five years old!

POA-POA and MING fade away.

Scene 13

>*SU-LING looks down at herself in the wedding finery. She starts tearing off her clothing, until she is only in her underthings.*

SU-LING: The reason that Nora leaves. The answer is, because, he doesn't know her at all.

>*A butterfly, and then the small feet of her mother. Projected text overlapping. SU-LING starts to unbind her feet. There is chaos around her, as if SU-LING is in the centre of a storm. She methodically and thoroughly opens her feet, pulling them in the opposite direction. She pulls outs reams and reams of unbound cotton.*

>*A lotus blossom, opening in the dawn. The suspended lotus shoes begin to rain down onto the set, littering everything. She collapses on her bed.*

Scene 14

>*An opium den. MERCHANT LI is floating, suspended.*

MERCHANT LI: Listen to me, Nora...

You don't know...

Your face so open...

Awakes my heart...

Like searing sunlight that lifts you...pains you all at once

I was hit, I inhaled...deeply, sharply

I suffered agonies...

I know...I concede...I cannot....

I am in surrender, Su-Ling. I surrender.

(Suddenly but gently aware of his surroundings.)

The war, it's over, isn't it...?

Scene 15

> *Early hours, still dark, SU-LING stirs from her delirium, covered in a blanket. Ming is standing over her.*

MING: I found you. You were passed out and all your wedding clothes, all your linens... They were everywhere.

SU-LING: Is tomorrow the wedding day?

MING: I made sure no one knew you were...sick.

SU-LING: I can't get married tomorrow.

MING: You'll be alright. I repaired and cleaned all the clothes. And your lotus shoes, I don't know how you did it...

> *SU-LING pulls up her blankets and takes off her slippers to reveal her malformed unbound feet.*

What have you done?

SU-LING: I took my lotus buds and I pried them open. I forced my feet to blossom.

MING: Chen won't marry you, with those deformed feet.

SU-LING: It doesn't matter...

MING: It's not too late. I can bind them properly and tight. No one will know.

SU-LING: I won't marry Chen.

MING:	What's wrong with you? Don't you know how many women would love to be in your position? You have a place to live, you have food, you have clothes!
SU-LING:	I want more.
MING:	Everyone wants more. But some people live with what they have.
SU-LING:	But I can't.
MING:	What? In this bed lined with silk! Fat dumplings for breakfast and servants at your beck and call! I was born next to pigs in the mud and the sick. But look at me. I've survived.
SU-LING:	It's not about survival!
MING:	What else is there?
SU-LING:	You're different than me.
MING:	You don't even know, you don't even realize! You forget about me as soon as I leave your room. But when the Chens see you on your wedding day, you will look perfect. Everything will be perfect. And they will know it was because of me!
SU-LING:	He killed that other concubine!
MING:	Only because she didn't mind her place!
SU-LING:	And if I don't? I'll end up like her! Burnt alive while the servants gawk! Why would I stay here?
MING:	Is it him? The merchant? Is that where you're going?
SU-LING:	No.
MING:	Then what are you going to do?
SU-LING:	It doesn't matter. I know that I can't stay.
MING:	You want to go? You want to just leave?
SU-LING:	I'll, I'll wear your clothes. And then I'll just walk away.

MING: But you can barely stand with your feet like this!

SU-LING: I'll manage! Give me your clothes, I'm going. Better to look like a servant.

SU-LING's starts taking off MING's outer clothing and putting it on.

MING: Do you know how many floors I had to clean. How many dishes I had to wash. How much kowtowing I had to do…

SU-LING: Help me up!

MING: Don't you get it? They will blame me!

SIU-LING: Tell them that you didn't know.

MING: They're not going to take away my job, they'll punish me! And I, I can't…I've lost enough already!

SU-LING: Then run away!

MING: I can't go! My mother and father already have scars on their backs.

SU-LING: I can't stay here.

An impasse.

MING: Hit me.

SU-LING: What?

MING: You would have to get past me. The Chens have to believe I'm innocent.

SU-LING: You try and stop me.

MING: But then you hit me, so I am unconscious and then…

SU-LING: Then I'm free to go! And you did all that you could.

MING: Yes… So. Hit me. Here. Take this. *(She hands her a wooden hairbrush.)* Come on.

SU-LING hesitates.

MING: It's not fair. If you're going to leave... You have to save me too. Hit me!

            SU-LING hits her across her face.

MING: *(Groaning.)* Ohhhh!

SU-LING: Ming...

MING: Again.

            SU-LING hits her again.

MING: *(Very weakly.)* Go.

            MING passes out from the pain and SU-LING leaves her on the floor.

Scene 16

            The courtyard outside SU-LING's room. POA-POA is waiting on the bench, carrying her cane. It is snowing.

SU-LING: Poa-Poa. I...I...

POA-POA: When we first moved here. I had such high hopes. Walls of plaster! And I thought, "good." But for days, they are all I see.

SU-LING: I have to go.

POA-POA: How many meals did I give up for you? The Chens will throw me into the street. I am old, and you will kill me.

SU-LING: How can you say that to me?

POA-POA: It's the truth.

SU-LING: You were one of Chen's servants. You were there. You were there when he began to punish the other concubine. Did you watch as he gagged her? As he poured alcohol down her throat? And when he lit the match! What did you do? And when she, when this girl was dead...what did you think? You thought...that he needed a new concubine! You thought that Chen needed a wife.

POA-POA: I had no choice. I wanted to give you a better life...

SU-LING: This is not life. I do not feel alive. This is only a world where I am constantly waiting. To be his plaything, picked up at his will, used and discarded. I will not stay here.

POA-POA: Everyone is always leaving me...everyone always leaves...

SU-LING: Goodbye, Poa-Poa.

POA-POA: Don't go. Not yet. Wait, please. My mother left me. My Ma-Ma. Tell me what she wrote on the letter.

SU-LING: The letter?

POA-POA: Where is it? The letter. From my mother.

SU-LING: I don't know... You burnt it.

POA-POA: I didn't. No I wouldn't do that. It's still here.

SU-LING: What do you mean?

POA-POA: Read it to me. Read it for an old lady.

SU-LING: I...I can't.

POA-POA: It's from my Ma-Ma. My mother, she wrote it for me. Before she died. What does it say?

SU-LING: I don't know.

POA-POA: Please. What does it say?

SU-LING: What does it say...it says. It says: Dear Tien-Mei.

POA-POA: No, no. My mother, my mother always called me Mei-Mei...

SU-LING: Uh...alright. Dear, dear Mei-Mei, I am writing to
                you from, from...

POA-POA: From her home village.

SU-LING: Dear Mei-Mei, I am writing to you from my home
                village. Forgive me. Forgive me because I had to
                leave you. I am so sorry for abandoning you. You
                must think that I don't love you. But it's not true. I
                love you, but I could not stay. I had to leave. And I
                know that you were alone. You were so lonely. But I
                also know that you are strong, my daughter. You are
                stronger than me. You will survive.

                *SU-LING tries to get to her feet. POA-POA hands
                SU-LING the cane as they look at each other for the
                last time. SU-LING leaves POA-POA and her
                thoughts in the courtyard. The snow stops, and sun
                comes with the dawn.*

Scene 17 Epilogue

> *In shadow, MA-MA and POA-POA echo their positions from Act I, Scene 1.*

MA-MA: *(Very low and far away.)*

Su-Ling-Ling. Who is smiling?

Su-Ling-Ling. Who is laughing?

Su-Ling-Ling. Who is walking?

> *Between them, SU-LING (16) walks painfully across the stage, excruciatingly slowly. She stumbles awkwardly. Using the cane for support, she gets slowly regains her feet, and begins to walk again, exiting the theatre space.*

> *The End.*

Timeline

	Historical Events	Events in the World of the Play
1867		Poa-Poa (Tien-Mei) born to Tian-Mei, a concubine.
1872		Poa-Poa's feet are bound.
1875	Political activist Qui-Jin is born.	
		Tian-Mei runs away, Poa-Poa stays in her father's house, adopted by the second wife. Merchant Li is born.
1880		Dying, Tian-Mei sends a letter to Poa-Poa.
1881		Poa-Poa marries Wang, later that year Ma-Ma (Hua-Ling) is born.
1886		Poa-Poa binds Ma-Ma's feet.
1894-5	Sino-Japanese War.	
1898		Ma-Ma marries Kuo, an opium addict and a gambler.
1900	Boxer Uprising.	Merchant Li leaves his village. Ming is born.
1902		Su-Ling born. Merchant Li returns to village.
1904		Su-Ling learns to walk.
1907	Sun-Yat Sen announces Chinese Democratic Republic Program.	
		Kuo overdoses. Ma-Ma commits suicide.
	Qui-Jin is beheaded.	Poa-Poa binds Su-Ling's feet.
1909		Poa-Poa and Su-Ling settle in Shanghai.
1911	Revolution forms Republic.	
		Su-Ling meets Merchant Li.
	Sun Yat-Sen elected president.	
1912	Sun Yat-Sen founds Kuomintang.	
		Su-Ling learns to read.
1914	WWI begins, Japan seizes Shandong province.	
		Su-Ling meets Ming for the first time.
1917	China enters WWI.	
Feb–1918		Poa-Poa and the Wongs discuss engagement.
Mar–1918		Su-Ling attempts to sew her engagement shoes. Second Son Chen acquires a concubine.
Apr–1918		Merchant Li sews Su-Ling's shoes for her. The Wongs reject Su-Ling because of her family.
July–1918		Soldier and concubine killed by the Chens.
Sept–1918		Su-Ling is engaged to Second Son Chen.
Oct–1918		Su-Ling and Poa-Poa move to the Chen compound.
Nov–1918	End of WWI.	Su-Ling unbinds her feet, and leaves Poa-Poa.